FOOD
AROUND THE WORLD

by
Joanna Brundle

Look out for green words in this book. You can find out what they mean in the Glossary on Page 24.

CONTENTS

We are going to visit lots of countries. Look at the map on Page 23 to find out where they are.

©2016
Book Life
King's Lynn
Norfolk PE30 4LS

ISBN: 978-1-78637-013-6

Written by:
Joanna Brundle

Designed by:
Natalie Carr

A catalogue record for this book is available from the British Library.

WHY DO WE EAT FOOD?

Around the world, everyone needs to eat food. Just like petrol in a car, food is the fuel that gives us energy and keeps our bodies working properly.

In order to be healthy, we need to eat different kinds of foods and to drink clean water.

LET'S SEE WHAT PEOPLE AROUND THE WORLD LIKE TO EAT.

TRADITIONAL FOODS

In the United Kingdom, many people enjoy fish and chips, especially at the seaside. Roast dinner is often eaten on Sundays.

FISH AND CHIPS

A FAMILY ENJOYING A ROAST DINNER TOGETHER

SUSHI

CHINESE FRIED NOODLES

In Asian countries, like China, people enjoy stir-fried rice and noodle dishes. Japanese people love sushi, made from sticky rice, vegetables and fish.

Italy is the home of pasta, pizza and delicious ice cream called gelato. Gelato is made in many different flavours including mango, black cherry and, of course, chocolate! What is your favourite flavour?

In Russia and Poland, soup called borscht is popular.
It is made from beetroot and served with rye bread.

RYE BREAD

9

Curry is the traditional food of India. Indian ice cream is called kulfi. It usually contains nuts.

CURRY

KULFI

SPICES USED TO FLAVOUR CURRIES

SPICY SAUCE CALLED SALSA

HOT CHILLI PEPPERS

In South American countries, like Mexico, people love eating tacos and tortillas filled with spicy meat, cheese and salad.

THE BIG THREE

MAIZE

WHEAT BEING HARVESTED IN THE USA

The three biggest food crops in the world are wheat, maize and rice. Wheat is turned into flour to make bread and cakes. Maize kernels can be eaten whole or ground into flour to make cornbread and tortillas.

Rice is eaten all over the world. The grains of rice are the seeds of the rice plant, which is a kind of grass.

SEEDS

RICE PLANTING IN THAILAND

FOOD AND RELIGIOUS FESTIVALS

CHRISTMAS PUDDING

STOLLEN CAKE

At Christmas, people in the United Kingdom enjoy Christmas pudding. Stollen cake is popular in Germany. At Easter, hot cross buns are eaten, to remember Jesus' death

14

At Diwali, a festival celebrated by Hindus and Sikhs, homemade sweets are eaten and given as gifts.

NUTS, RAISINS AND COCONUT ARE SOME OF THE INGREDIENTS USED TO MAKE THE SWEETS.

FASTING

DATES

In Muslim countries, like Indonesia, people fast during the holy month of Ramadan. In the evening, they stop fasting by eating dates.

Families and friends then gather together and enjoy a special meal called iftar. It is eaten with pitta bread.

PITTA BREAD

IFTAR MEAL

WHERE DO PEOPLE GET FOOD?

A FRUIT MARKET IN KENYA

CAKES FROM FRANCE

People buy food from street markets as well as supermarkets and specialist shops like butchers and fishmongers. France is famous for beautiful cake shops.

Amazon Indians hunt for different types of deer and monkey in the rainforest. The Bajau people of Borneo dive down twenty metres to catch fish in the sea.

THESE FISHERMEN IN SRI LANKA BALANCE ON STILTS TO SPEAR FISH.

19

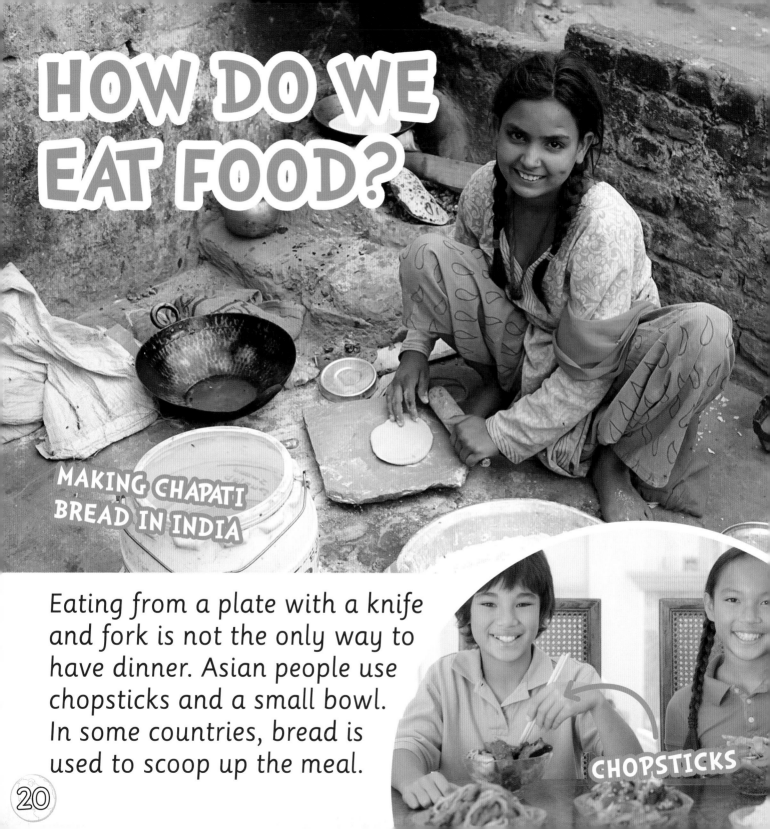

HOW DO WE EAT FOOD?

MAKING CHAPATI BREAD IN INDIA

Eating from a plate with a knife and fork is not the only way to have dinner. Asian people use chopsticks and a small bowl. In some countries, bread is used to scoop up the meal.

CHOPSTICKS

Many foods are eaten with our fingers, like sandwiches and fruits. In Greece and Turkey, vine leaves are used to wrap rice and meat to make dolmades.

A PLATE OF DOLMADES

HUNGER

Many people around the world do not have enough to eat. Some people, even though they live in wealthy countries like the USA, do not have enough money for food. Food banks help by offering free food, which has been given by other people and supermarkets.

THIS BOY IS LOOKING FOR FOOD ON A RUBBISH DUMP.

A FOOD BANK

WHERE IN THE WORLD?

1. England
2. China
3. Japan
4. Italy
5. France
6. Greece
7. Turkey
8. USA
9. Thailand
10. Germany
11. Indonesia
12. Russia
13. Poland
14. India
15. Mexico
16. Kenya
17. Borneo
18. Sri Lanka
19. Ethopia

1. Europe
2. North America
3. South America
4. Africa
5. Australia
6. Asia
7. Amazon Rain Forest

23

GLOSSARY

FAST To stop eating food

FUEL Something that gives energy or power

INGREDIENTS Food items that are put together to make a meal

VINE The grape plant

WEALTHY Having lots of money

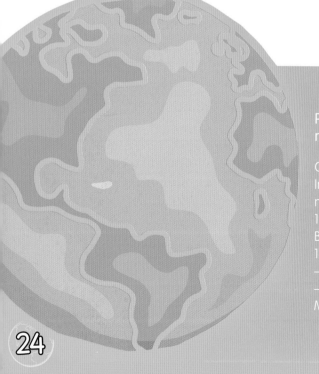